LESSONS
FROM
ROCKY

BRADFORD P. MILLER

Outskirts Press, Inc.
Denver, Colorado

Lessons From Rocky
All Rights Reserved
Copyright © 2007 Bradford Putnam Miller
V2.0

Outskirts Press
http://www.outskirtspress.com

ISBN-10: 1-4327-0210-6
ISBN-13: 978-1-4327-0210-6

Library of Congress Control Number: 2006939112

Outskirts Press and the "OP" logo are trademarks belonging to Outskirts Press, Inc.

Printed in the United States of America

TABLE OF CONTENTS

ACKNOWLEDGEMENTS

This book is dedicated to my wife, Pam, who was with me every step of the way, sharing her nuggets of wisdom. She believed in me, supported my efforts, and cheered me on at each stage of accomplishment. I thank you so much for your faith.

To our wonderful dog Rocky, who has left his legacy chronicled within these pages. His courage, joy, happiness, and unending friendship have become part of the fabric of our being.

To our good friends who read my manuscript and offered their valuable insights, encouragement, and support about the importance of completing this book and getting it into the hands of those who would benefit from Rocky's wisdom. They are Deacon Cecie Titcomb and Elise Moloney from Bethesda-By-The-Sea Church, Susanna Walker from Hospice of Palm Beach County, Florida, my two sisters,

Deborah Lalor and Constance Bergh whose love of pets was so freely shared with me, Brooke Emery who was a lighthouse on the horizon,

Barbara (Bobbi) Rae, whose insights helped clear the fog and our dear friend Sherrill Whetsell who provided so much support.

Thank you all for being a part of my life.

BEFORE THE FOREWORD

I have written this book for three reasons.

The first is for the benefit of animal lovers whose pets are still with them. I wanted to share with you the wonderful lessons I learned from my little dog. He was an amazing character, and although I learned a lot from him during our years together when his life was so vibrant, it wasn't until after he had passed away that I truly appreciated everything he had taught me. It is for that reason that I share my thoughts in the hope that every day you will stop long enough to appreciate all the wonders of your pet. When you are running out the door with no time to spare and just as the door closes you see THAT look in their eyes, STOP, don't miss that moment. They are *all* so fleeting, and they are limited. I guarantee that you will never regret the extra moments you take to look deep into those beautiful eyes and share your love with them. It is in that irretrievable moment of time between doing all the activities in your life that true life and happiness exists. I hope you will take that special moment to return the love that is being given to you unconditionally.

The second reason is because I truly wanted to share with you all the wonderful lessons I had learned from Rocky. It's not like I had never thought or felt what I was going through, but after he had passed away, it was as if I saw and felt emotions in a new way. My feelings had a newer, fresher tone, and my level of appreciation had been elevated. Even as I write this now, I can only surmise that the legacy he left is just an extension of the gifts he passed on to me.

The third reason this book has been written is a selfish one, I must confess. In the past, before Rocky passed away, I had pondered how I might feel when the inevitable came to pass. What I discovered was none of us ever truly knows how we will feel when a loved one passes away, human or animal. I have experienced the loss of grandparents, parents, friends, and pets. Each time was emotional and each time, different. If someone ever tells you that losing a pet is not the same as losing a relative or friend, then perhaps they have never been blessed with knowing the fulfillment of companionship and the bond of love that a pet brings into our lives. It is because of my unique feelings (yours are unique also) that I write this book for cathartic reasons. It has helped me crystallize the moments of my life with Rocky. By sharing this with you, I hope you will appreciate your furry friend that much more today, and if they have passed away, find solace in my words. Please visit our website www.lessonsfromrocky.com for more information.

FOREWORD

On August 7, 2006 our little dog, Rocky, a mixed-breed terrier from the Humane Society, passed away. It was such a sad day, however, one that we had been anticipating for a long time. Somehow we mortals think we can determine how we will feel when a pet passes away, but it isn't until that moment that the reality sinks in that your little friend will not be with you anymore.

It comes at you like a tidal wave of emotion, unexpected. No matter how much you think you are prepared, there is no way to tell how YOU will feel when the moment comes. They're your feelings, and nobody can understand the special bond that you have with your dog or cat or other pet. Nobody can understand all the special moments that you shared. If you were to take all the moments in your life of things that happened to you and then add the component of your furry friend, you will see how often they were a part of the experience. Only you will be able to understand the loss to the full extent.

So here I sit with the memory of Rocky, The Amazing Dog. As I reflected on our loss and felt the grief and sadness well up inside me, tears started flowing from my eyes. The pain in my heart of realizing that I would never see my little friend again brought wave upon wave of despair. I was feeling so sorry for myself, and then something clicked inside me. Rocky may not be with me here on earth, but he will always be in my heart and in my mind. I started to think of what I had learned from Rocky over the last 17 years. As my thoughts collected, I realized that I wanted to share all I had learned from him with you. At the same time, my hope was that by sharing these "Lessons from Rocky", anyone reading this who had also lost a pet would think about what they had learned from their pet. Like history, we want to learn from other's experiences, so I share.

My hope is that if you have lost a pet and are feeling the sadness of that loss, by reading this book with love in your heart, you, too, will remember all the things you learned from your wonderful pet and how valuable that memory is to you.

Today, as I reflect about Rocky, I still can see his happy face in my mind's eye, and I immediately think of all the positive things that he taught me. I hope that as you read through this book, it will help in quelling the sadness you must be feeling. My prayers and thoughts go out to you at this very sad time and hope that you find the relief you seek.

PROLOGUE

It all seems so surreal now as I look back and remember the 17 years that we spent together. When you were young you were so vibrant and alive, and then, almost imperceptibly your energy waned as the years passed. I could not put my finger on any one thing, but looking back now I can see the pattern of your passing years. Things you stopped doing, like your wonderful 180 and 360 degree spin circles you used to perform for us, or how you carried your favorite doggie bone in your teeth pointing straight out. How clever was that? But you had stopped doing those things and replaced them with other equally wonderful antics, but less stressful on you. I know the bones became too hard for you to chew, so we replaced them with softer ones. Little by little we had to change what worked for you, and we were so happy to do anything for you that would make you feel more comfortable. In a semi state of denial we watched as your health declined. The doctor said it was just a matter of time. Finally, you couldn't swallow anymore, and the look in your eyes kept saying, "I'm here for you, whatever you need I will do. I am here to comfort you and stand by you and love you and protect you, but I just can't get up right now." We knew, and we loved you for never giving up.

Now, looking back at all our years together, I can see with such great clarity how you taught us so much about life and about ourselves. I realize now that you never gave up on us, even when we were so slow to learn. You lived the life that we wish we had been living. One day at a time, in the moment, as if nothing else mattered in the world.

With great joy in my heart, I now carry your lessons with me. Every day I know I will call on one of my "Lessons from Rocky" and smile, knowing that all along you knew how to live a full and happy life.

CHAPTER 1

LOSING YOUR BEST FRIEND

"Slowly, gradually, he detached himself, breathing less and less, fainter and fainter; then was he off and free, like a dry leaf from the tree, floating down and away." —Helen Nearing (1904-1995)
Loving and Leaving the Good Life

The ticking of the grandfather clock in the front hall was the only sound heard in the house. The air was so still. I don't think I can remember a time when it was so quiet.

My ears were cocked, waiting for that familiar sound, but nothing was heard except the still empty silence and the ticking of the clock... tick... tick... tick... tick... tick...

Perpetual, each tick a pain in my heart signaling the loss that was so profound and deep, and leaving a hole so empty that infinite space seemed to feel full in comparison to the void I felt.

This wasn't fair. Nobody had warned me that I would feel so alone or that I would have such an incredible flood of emotions and despair...why this aching in my heart, which would surface in an instant and before I knew or expected anything, I would be crying. Involuntarily, the tears would flood from my eyes; there was no reason to hold back. I just let it go, and after a time they would stop, only to resurface later.

"Backward, turn backward, O time in your flight;
Make me a child again just for tonight." —Elizabeth Akers Allen,
Rock Me to Sleep

My mind drifted off again, and all I could hear was the tick...tick...ticking of the clock.

Why am I feeling so guilty? I feel as though I should have spent more time with him. But I did spend time with him. I played with him, scratched his head. We would sit on the sofa together for hours. He would always sit right next to me, the warmth of his body like a little heater; his rhythmic breathing matching mine as if we were one soul. The universe had taken two stars and put us together, and like the rising and setting of the sun and moon, we were living our lives in perfect harmony. In the morning he was the first thing I thought of as I rolled over. He was my child that never grew up. I had to let him out to take care of his business. If I was eating, he had to eat, and he never had any trouble reminding me to fill his bowl. He loved his little treats and was always so enthusiastic that it was difficult not to give him an extra one. He got everything he wanted, and I was happy to give it to him because he gave so much back to me. Unconditionally with love, joy, and happiness, he gave of himself with no thought of reward.

Did I hear something in the breakfast room? Nooo, I guess it wasn't anything. Just my mind wishing it was the sound of his toenails on the floor and his familiar breathing as he came around the corner. I so wish this feeling of emptiness would go away. So many things that we did together. I feel so alone right now. Not a sound. I think I'll just sit here and think. Think about all the moments we shared. I loved it when he put his head on my lap and looked up at me with his big brown eyes. I'll just close my eyes and see his beautiful face. That's it, think and listen and listen and listen to the...tick...tick...ticking of the clock.

CHAPTER 2

A DREAM

"Our truest life is when we are in dreams awake." —Henry David Thoreau (1817-1862). *"Wednesday" A Week on the Concord and Merrimack Rivers, 1849*

Rocky!!!! What are you doing here? I...I...I...thought you had, well, died...forget that...you're here, here with me, and we're together again. A team. Reunited. I can't believe it's you. I knew you wouldn't leave me. Come here so I can hold you and scrunch you in my arms. Boy, do you smell good. You must have gotten an amazing bath. Heavenly, you say. Well, you always loved your baths. What did you say? It was the most fantastic bath you ever had. Well, I guess in Heaven you would get a pretty good coif! Well, you deserve the best of everything.

I have so much to tell you. Just in our short separation I realize how much I had learned from you over the last 17 years. That's right; we've been together for 17 years. Let's see, in dog years that would make you, 7 X 17 = 119 years old. What did you say... Boy, you're right, you were a year old when you came to live with us... So...that makes you, 119 + 7 = 126 years old. Rocky, for someone as old as you are, you sure didn't act your age. OK, OK, I only mean that in the nicest way. WOW! 126 years old. You truly deserved all those yummy dog treats we gave you!!!

You know, Rocky, I was feeling so lonely without you, and I was having all these emotions because you were no longer with me, but I started to think of all the things I had learned from you and realized that you have been my best teacher ever. What did I learn from you? Well, come over here and sit in my lap the way you used to, and let's just share this special time together like we used to. I just can't believe you're here with me right now. I don't want to waste a moment.

CHAPTER 3

LOVE

"Love bears all things, believes all things, and hopes all things." —Paul, 1 Corinthians 13:4-7

*E*veryone I have ever talked to can remember in the finest detail the exact moment they met their pet. It's a moment that has been preserved in time like a fossil from the Ice Age. Many times I hear people say that they picked their pet at the Humane Society or the pet store, but I don't think WE pick our pets at all. I think THEY pick us, or even more so, we have been selected to be together by a power that is greater than all of us. No matter how it is that we have ended up together, there is a bond that is created at that moment, which will endure through all time. Savor the moments, for they are all so fleeting.

Rocky, do you remember when you first met us? That's right, at Dwight and Keithley's house in St. Louis. They had too many dogs and cats, and you were going to be heading to a new home. As fate would have it, in walks Pam and Brad. Do you remember that? I know, how could you forget it. Knowing your fate was hanging in the balance and seeing opportunity, you ran across their kitchen and took a leap of faith into Pam's arms as she was sitting at the kitchen table. Using your best manners, you gave her a long, deep look in her eyes that said, "Take me, I'm yours," and then gave her a big lick on the cheek. It was the perfect sales pitch, and you handled it masterfully. Pam looked at me with her beautiful blue eyes, asking if we could take you home with us. Our wonderful Wheaton terrier, Corky, had died a year earlier, and there was an emptiness in our lives. Knowing how much Pam missed Corky, I gave her the yes nod, and like magic we were a family. Yes, Rocky, it was a magical moment; I remember it like it was yesterday. You wiggled in 100 different directions all at once, confirming to us that we had made the right decision. You were special the first day and every day after that. You were the best, best, best friend we ever had. You brought incredible happiness into our lives, and for that we will always be grateful and remember how you gave us so much love.

You taught us so much about love and the meaning of unconditional love. No matter what was going on, you were there to lighten the moment. We were so serious back then. Everything seemed so important in our business and our life, but no matter what, you would always, no exception, always be there to comfort us in our time of need. If we came home exhausted from the office, you would curl up next to us on the sofa and just be there for us. I appreciate that so much today. You never turned your back on us. At bedtime you were always there. You have the most gentle and wise eyes. It's like you understood everything that we said. I will say that you always managed to establish a very strategic beachhead on the bed. Over the years you had your pick of wherever you wanted to sleep. As Pam reminded me, for years you started sleeping next to her, but by morning you had moved over and were giving me a full body hug. You were really good at those. Now that I think of it, there was never a night that you didn't sleep on our bed. That's a pretty good record.

Because of you, Rocky, we have a new understanding of unconditional love. You truly understand love, and I find great peace in that thought. Recently we learned to look at all people and say, "The beauty I see in you is..." I now know that everyone has beauty in them and that it is up to me to look and see it. We now take the time to listen to people and hear what it is they are saying. When I look at other people with love in my heart, I see all their beauty. It is a gift from you that I will always cherish. Thank you. Thank you from the bottom of my heart. Thank you.

CHAPTER 4

TRUST

"Who is the wise man? He who sees what's going to be born." Solomon

*T*hink how much trust is required by all of us on a daily basis. I believe each of us has a choice as to how each day is going to go. When we get out of bed, our thoughts are what determine the outcome of the day. Whether you see your glass as **half full or half empty**...you're right. Whether you believe that you **can** or **can not**...you're right, and whether you believe that you **will** or **will not** have all that you need on a daily basis...you're right.

Do you realize, Rocky, that on any given day you didn't know whether you were going to be fed breakfast or dinner? Yeah, I guess you did know that. Well, you got me thinking about trust and the amount of trust you had every day because you didn't know whether food would be served to you or not. I had to learn how to trust other people, and when I think of trust, I think of you. Well, you were 99% good at trust. Just to make sure you were fed, you would sometimes have to remind us in your own special way. You were really funny. You would walk over to your bowl and stand over it until we finally got the message. You must have known that we had the look that we might forget to feed you, like when we were in a rush to get out the door in the morning. I think in all our years together, we never missed a feeding time, which is pretty amazing. OK, with your help we never missed. Well, we made a good team. We would fix the dinner, and you would eat.

OK, let's not get into the quality issue. The vet told us what to feed you because that's what was good for you.

You also became an excellent table beggar. When it was just the three of us, I didn't mind so much, and when we said no more, you were usually very good at stopping. Yeah, you really loved the BBQ chicken, cookies, and occasional nibble of chocolate. Chocolate is not good for you; that's why we never gave very much. I will say there wasn't much you wouldn't eat off the plate except vegetables. Well, considering the variety of food that you did consume over your 126 years, I would say that you did pretty well for yourself.

Rocky, I am so glad you're here. It is so great to talk to you and tell you about all the things that were on my mind. Love and trust. You can't live without them in the world today. Thank you my friend.

CHAPTER 5

JOY

"All animals except man know that the principal business of life is to enjoy it."
—Samuel Butler

*H*ave you ever thought to yourself how is it that your fabulous furry creature could have come into your life and without training of any kind and without anyone to instruct them, have so much joy in their heart? As you think of your bundle of joy, have you thought to yourself "I need to have more joy in my life"? We can all learn from others, but most of all, look to your pets for guidance, because THEY have figured it out.

Rocky the Amazing. You know, that's what I loved to call you. You showed us so much about joy. I can close my eyes and see the joy you had for the exact moment you were living in. As Ralph Waldo Emerson said, **"Allow yourself to trust joy and embrace it. You will find you dance with everything."**

Do you remember when we were living on Fordyce Lane in St. Louis? I think it was the first autumn that we had moved there. The foliage was so colorful, so many hues of oranges and reds and browns. It was beautiful to walk around the lane and smell the sweet smell of autumn. You were...yes, amazing! The piles of leaves recently raked became your playground. You would race down the street and, take a joyful leap into the leaf piles. You were so excited to disappear into a pile, only to reappear on the other side. Joy, pure joy!!! Then we would jump in the piles with you, and you would jump on top of us. You loved it, and the joy in your smile told the whole story. You were loving and appreciating every moment of your life. You taught us to savor the moment and to have joy. I also remember how you would disappear into the woods and come darting out 50 or 100 yards away from where you entered. You thought that was so cool. It was. You would be running along and then spontaneously you would leap five feet high in the air. We would always be amazed at how high you could jump. Your energy was contagious.

Do you remember when you discovered that small stream in the middle of the woods? You must have really loved to smell yucky. The mud in that stream was truly foul, but it didn't stop you from rolling in it from time to time. Now that I think of it, that must have been your way of letting me know you needed a bath. Well, you still did it with joy, because after you had gotten yourself perfectly covered in the black muck, you would race toward us with such incredible exuberance and glee. You loved it, didn't you? I think you're smiling at me.

Thank you for showing us pure joy. Pure joy, where you let it all hang out. This is life. No dress rehearsal, so you better get with it and let the joy out. We got the joy, and joy is part of our life. Rocky, you are a great teacher!

CHAPTER 6

LOYALTY

"Loyalty is reciprocal." —Richard E. Neustadt (1919-) from *Presidential Power: The Politics of Leadership*

*C*lose *your eyes after you have read this short passage and reflect on the steadfast loyalty you have experienced with your pet. How special to bask in the glow, knowing that you have a partner who, regardless of anything, is there for you no matter what, through thick and thin, whatever might come. Whenever you hear someone say, "I've got your back," remember that nobody ever had your back more than your pet. As you close your eyes and take a long gentle breath through your nose, think how much that loyalty has meant to you over all the years and how special the experience was to you.*

You know, Rocky, when we were united, neither us took an oath, but as I look back, you adhered to the concept of loyalty as if you had been sworn in as the President of the United States. What does it mean? It means maintaining allegiance, steadfast, bound by an oath; duty or obligation. That's the dictionary's definition. My definition is, you were my best friend.

If you sensed that someone was not a good person, you let them know by exhibiting your best growl and bark. I remember strangers coming to our house or office, and you would always give them the sniff test. If you gave a growl or bark, I learned to heed your good judgment and kept an eye on them. From the sound of your bark, you would have laid your life down to protect our lives. That is loyalty. I always felt that you were 100% dedicated to us, and your steadfast allegiance earned my respect. That's right, Rocky, I respected you all those years and you knew it, didn't you? Don't go fishing for compliments now. You got plenty of them over the years. OK, you were the best dog ever, ever, ever.

We thank you. You were loyal to us in all senses of the word, and you taught us the importance of being loyal to friends and family and spouses. I know you never even considered leaving us. Why would you? We were having so much fun. You are my very loyal friend.

CHAPTER 7

CELEBRATION

"To be alive, to be able to see, to walk...it's all a miracle. I have adapted the technique of living life from miracle to miracle." —Arthur Rubinstein

I love to watch sporting events because of all the celebrations after each mini victory (the score) and at the end of a competition when the winner goes crazy with jubilation. I will endure hours of tennis, golf, football, baseball, basketball, motorcross, skiing, volleyball, and even curling just to see the elation of the participants at that quintessential moment of Victory. That euphoric microcosmic moment that victory is sealed. There is no better moment that so perfectly exemplifies people's true emotions.

Now when we talk about pets, well, that's a different story because you never have to wait to see a real celebration. Pets celebrate EVERYTHING! Think about it.
If you pick up their leash...they celebrate!
Time for dinner? Big celebration!
Do you want to play in the yard? You got it... Celebration time again!
Have you learned to celebrate EVERYTHING?

Do you mind if I move you around a little bit on my lap? Ahhh, that's better.

I used to look at you in amazement and wonder how you managed to get so excited about so many things. You celebrated everything in your life. I think you lived your life as if every day was a miracle, and you looked at everything you did as if it would never happen again. Your unending curiosity, which led you to places I would never dream of going, is exactly what made your life so interesting. You would follow a lizard into the bushes, and all we would hear was you routing around in there, only to appear at the other end of the hedge with that triumphant look on your face. You were always respectful to check in with us to let us know that everything was OK, and then you would be off for your next exploration.

"Rocky, let's go for a walk." You would jump up and down like you were on a trampoline. Anyone else would look at your circus act and might think this was the first time you had ever been on a walk. You had this incredible way that you could jump and spin around at the same time, and then of course you would bark with glee at the prospect that we would be going for a walk. You celebrated the moment, and the prospect of that was such a source of happiness for you. Every day was truly a miracle for you, and we had the pleasure of sharing it with you.

I also loved to watch you first beg for a bone, and when you knew you would get one, you would celebrate. Jump. Bark. Jump. Bark. It was always the same and always entertaining. You saw the magic in every moment!

In your younger days, you could have qualified for the Olympic high jump and long jump. When it was time for bed, you would race to the top of the stairs and wait until we had caught up with you and then make a beeline down the hall to the bedroom, where you would spring in the air and land on the bed. Your score for height and distance should go down in the record books. I'll bet if I had measured it, it would have been at least ten feet. Once on the bed, the real celebration began. Jumping in circles and barking to show us how proud you were of your achievement. You really knew how to celebrate.

One of your greatest celebrations was when we were driving in the car and you would put your head out the window. Pam had to get a good hold on your collar because she was sure you thought you could fly and would have jumped right out the window at the first sight of another dog.

I'll bet you felt like you were flying when you did that, right? Yeah, I love the wind in my face, too.

I also remember how you loved to chase the squirrels. When you were younger, you were pretty fast and would get right up behind them. They always managed to find the nearest tree, but it was always entertaining to watch you dart back and forth across the neighbors' lawns in your quest to harass the lowly squirrel.

You have shown me that I need to celebrate everything in my life because everything that I do should be celebrated. Yeah, I get it now, but I didn't for so long, so I have some catching up to do. The good news is that I can still go back in time and congratulate myself on so many of my past successes.

What kind of successes am I going to celebrate? Well, for example, when I have a list of things that I need to do, I need to celebrate each and everything that I complete on the list. Even if I only finish part of something, I'm going to celebrate even getting started on the task. Success begets success, and the more I celebrate, the more success I will have. From now on, I will only focus on my success. When I walk a mile...success. If I have a house project that I do and I complete it ...success. Everything in life is about success. Why not celebrate all the time? The truth is, nobody else is going to celebrate my successes, so from now on I'm going to do it for myself. Every day. Matter of fact, Rocky, from now on, before I go to bed at night, I'm going to write down five successes that I had that day. That way I will truly appreciate the successes I do have, no matter how small.

Thank you, my dear old friend, for teaching me how to celebrate every day with enthusiasm. It brings joy to my heart, and I will always credit you with opening my eyes to the joy of celebration.

CHAPTER 8

PATIENCE

"They, who wait for the Lord, shall renew their strength, they shall mount up with wings like eagles, they shall run and not be weary, they shall walk and not faint." —ISAIAH (8th Century BC) Isaiah 40.13

*H*ave you ever wondered what your pet was doing all day while you were at work or out shopping? Have you ever felt that pang of guilt when just as you were heading out the door, they gave you a look that would break a heart? Did you ever say to yourself that you were going to spend more time with them when you got a chance? Well, your chance is now. Now is the time because now is the only time we have. Yesterday is gone and tomorrow isn't here, so live life today as if it were the last day you had to live. Imagine how precious every moment will feel and how respectful you will be of the time you have.

This has not been easy for me. I've always thought to myself, "I want what I want, when I want it, AND...I WANT IT NOW! That's the human being in me talking. No surprise to you.

But as to real patience, you were an expert.

We would leave for work in the morning, and you would go to your bed in the kitchen or the little tool room outside the kitchen, which had the doggy door...you liked that doggy door, didn't you? I thought so. You waited all day long for us to return. You were patient, and you had amazing trust that we would return. After we moved to Florida and you didn't have your little doggy door anymore, you really exhibited amazing bladder control and patience. In all the years you never...well, hardly ever had a mistake in the house. I know, we really tested your plumbing.

But the wonderful thing was that you waited patiently all day long, and when we returned, no matter how late, you weren't angry or fussy, you were happy to see us. You celebrated with your eyes and ears and bark and wiggle and showed us how much you missed us. God, you are so wonderful.

Now I miss you so much, and as I think about patience, I realize that I have learned so much of it from you. Like what? Well now, I accept what is...and I utilize what comes to me no matter what form. I may want a certain outcome right now, but if it doesn't happen right now or the way I want it or think I want it, I don't fret about it anymore. It is what it is and that's OK. When I think that something should happen faster than it does, I now stop and think how you sat patiently on your little pillow. You trusted that the right things would happen in your life and that you would get everything that you needed; and you did. No stress. You stopped and smelled the roses and allowed the universe to move at the speed it chose.

I have learned so much from you, my dear friend.

I no longer have to be first in line. What a stupid thing that is. Sometimes you don't even know what you're lining up for, and sometimes the beginning of the line becomes the end. You just kind of never know what's going to happen next. So now I can practice my patience, and when I do, I think of you sitting patiently on your pillow until we get home.

Thank you for this incredible lesson.

CHAPTER 9

COURAGE

"A wound, a red badge of courage." —
Stephen Crane (1871-1900) *The Red Badge
of Courage*

*H*ave you ever had a pet that was injured or sick? Did you feel helpless as you watched them in pain and having them looking up at you and not being able to tell you how much it hurt and why can't you make the pain go away? Have you held them in your arms and felt how the life in them had ebbed or was so much less than what it was before? This is the time that they need your energy to revitalize them. Hold them close and help them to regenerate the life energy that they have lost.

I will never forget that day in October when the neighbor's mean dog attacked you. Let's see, you weighed 20 pounds, and he weighed 125 pounds. We were visiting Bill and Ellie at their newly finished home just three houses from ours on Fordyce Lane. It was a beautiful day, and we were all walking around the exterior of the house when the neighbor's dog came over. He looked friendly and nobody really noticed him until...

I have never heard a dog make the crying, yelping, and screaming sounds that you did. I knew instantly that this was a life or death attack. The dog had you on your back and was chewing and biting his way up your stomach from your back legs to your neck, where he bit into your neck, picked you up, and whipped you around from side to side like you were a rag doll. It happened in less than 20 seconds, but the damage to you was critical. I started chasing him and kicked him in the stomach three or four times just to get him away from you. Then he stopped and looked at me like I was to be his next target. Just then his owner showed up and kept saying his dog would never attack another dog, and he didn't know how the dog got out. We later found out that the dog was a habitual runner and had gotten into trouble before. In addition to that, they had to use two Invisible fence collars and that still wouldn't keep the dog in his own yard. We reported the incident to the police. The owners were mad because if a dog had three incidents in our town, it meant the dog had to be put down because they were a danger to society. I could have cared less. We weren't sure if you were going to live, and that was all I cared about.

Do you remember that time, Rocky? OK, you can show me the scars again. It sure was scary, wasn't it? You were so courageous. You kept trying to get up, but you were in really bad shape. Pam finally got to you and picked you up. Your stomach was all chewed up, and blood was coming out of your belly in several places. As soon as we were with you, you knew you would be OK, didn't you? The rest is history; you did recover beautifully, even though it took several weeks. You used to lie on the family room sofa on your back. You were a very good patient. You also became the local radar for that mean dog. If he walked past our driveway, you would let out a low guttural sound and then bark like crazy. Your nose has an amazing sensor, and your heart is the size of the universe. You had such great courage that day, and I have locked that moment in my heart to remember that I can do anything with courage.

CHAPTER 10

CURIOSITY

"[They] are indolent discoverers, who seeing nothing but sea and sky, absolutely deny there can be any land beyond them." —Francis Bacon (1561-1626) *Advancement of Learning*

*H*ow do you see the world? Do you see through your own eyes and are inhibited by the barriers that we have placed in front of us, or have you trained yourself to look beyond our own barriers and yearn to see that which has not yet revealed itself? When we walk down our road and the road curves ahead, do you stop yourself from imagining what is to come, or do you challenge your thinking to imagine what might be? I see and hear people every day verbalize what can't be done because... What is **your** thought process? Does the mountain range on the horizon signal the end, or is it a challenge to imagine what lies beyond? Our pets live in a personal world of new discovery. Like a child experimenting with the world around him, pets are on a perpetual journey of discovery, there to remind us that we, too, are just visitors here and are responsible for looking beyond our own little world. Don't miss this amazing opportunity to exercise your curiosity.

You know, Rocky, from the day we met, you have always been the same curious little creature. Everything in the world interested you. Like what? OK, for instance, you would always come out to sit by the pool with us. You never sat very long because there was a world to explore in our backyard. Everything interested you. The geckos were always your first interest. In the beginning, you would sit motionless, watching the little lizards, and then ever so slowly you would start to move toward one of them. They would disappear in a heartbeat. As time went on, you never gave up in your quest to catch one, and I think your curiosity must have continued to hold your interest about them. They still catch my attention, and I think of you and the time you spent watching them.

I also remember vividly how you wandered around the different yards that we have had over the years. I would look up from the book I was reading, and you would be sniffing around the bushes, a tree, or even the edge of the house. Everything you did was of interest to you. You loved the world of discovery and in turn made my life more interesting. I now look at the world with a new set of eyes. I try to see beyond what is right in front of me to the curve in the road. No fear, just curiosity. Thank you.

CHAPTER 11

LIVING IN THE MOMENT

"Let me tell thee, time is a very precious gift of God, so precious that it is only given to us moment by moment." — Amelia Barr

Y ou would think that something as basic as living in the moment wouldn't require any thought at all, **but it really does.** *I think as humans we need to be reminded about living in today all the time, and that includes being reminded about living in the NOW. How often during your busy day are you thinking of what might have happened yesterday or projecting out to tomorrow about some meeting that you dread? Have you ever done that? Amazingly, in your mind you have already decided that the outcome of tomorrow is not going to be good, and you then proceed to worry about the outcome until the next day, only to find out that everything had changed and, in fact, the outcome was exactly what you wanted but were too afraid to think about. Close your eyes and see yourself living in this moment. Listen to the sounds around you; take a good sniff and appreciate the aromas that surround us. This is the only time you have. Right NOW! Enjoy it because it is so very special.*

Rocky, you were a master at living in the now. I can see you on your daily trip to the backyard. If there was a nice breeze, you would stand there, point your nose in the direction of the breeze, and just enjoy the moment. It was such a beautiful sight to see you making it yours. For that moment in time you owned the breeze.

You also used to lie on your back in the grass and wiggle back and forth. You were so happy in your moment, and I used to delight in just watching as you appreciated that moment. I remember one time after you had been wiggling in the grass (OK, you were scratching your back), you stopped and were still. Something had caught your attention or you were just stopping for a minute, but you were in a very special moment, and I was amazed at how still you were. You taught me the value in stopping and appreciating the moment. I'm not an expert at it, but every day I make a point of just stopping. Thank you for that wonderful lesson.

Do you remember all our walks to the beach? You loved the beach but just weren't that excited about the water. When we were in the water swimming, you would race back and forth, barely avoiding the incoming surf. After a time you would stop and just watch us, but as I looked at you, you were also watching the clouds drift by.

You were in your moment. I'd even say you were in a Zen moment.

I am taking those moments and I'm putting them in that little compartment in my mind labeled, "Living in the Moment." If I ever get too much with the world, racing hither and yon, I will be able to go revisit that place and remember what is really important in life, just the way you showed me.

Thank you for putting the simple things in life in perspective. You have given me so many wonderful lessons, and living in the moment, living in the NOW is so important and valuable. If I live in the moment, then I can't be thinking about yesterday, which is gone, and I can't speculate on tomorrow because it isn't here. If I live in this very moment, that is the essence of life. Right now!

CHAPTER 12

HAPPINESS

"All I can say about life is, Oh God, enjoy it!" —Bob Newhart

*H*ave you ever had someone say to you, "You should be happy"? I suppose we should all be happy just to be alive. I look around and I think I see people who are happy, but then they don't act happy. The publisher/author William Feathers said, **"Plenty of people miss their share of happiness, not because they didn't find it, but because they didn't take the time to enjoy it."**

Take a minute and think about what has really made you happy in the last week, month, or year. Overall, happiness is not found in how much money or things we accumulate but rather in special moments that are shared with others. Have you ever noticed that people who have more than ample resources end up giving their money away, getting involved in charitable ventures, or giving their time to organizations in need? What they have discovered is that true happiness comes to us when we are giving of ourselves. If it was money and riches that made us happy, we would just work more and more so we could have more money. ***But, that's not how it works.***

Now is a great time to think about everything around you, including your pet.

What makes them happy? What makes you happy? ENJOY IT!

Rocky, I can say, unequivocally, you knew what true happiness was and you took the time to be in your happy moments. It was in your walk, your skip, and your hop. It was in your eyes and the way they sparkled and looked at us, telling us every day that this was a great day. Today, right now.

Well, now that you ask, we were remembering all your happy moments, and they **ALL** are very special.

You loved parties. Whenever we had friends over, you wanted to be included. You were the original party animal and would happily stop to greet anyone willing to give you a friendly scratch on the head. I know, you were a little beggar also and conned your fair share of food.

You loved to get your baths. After a bath, you would race around the house jumping and shaking and trying to get dry by rolling around on everything. You especially loved to shake until you would almost lose your balance. Yeah! You were really good at it.

You were happy when we took you to the office. Every time, you would race around from office to office to see who was there. It was new to you every time, and you always looked so happy to be included. Matter of fact, any time we would say, "Rocky, car," you would do your jump and circles routine just to show us how happy you were to be included in the next adventure.

You made the best of every moment, and you were happy in your moment. How great is that to just be happy. Right now. It's not about yesterday or tomorrow. It's about right now and deciding to be happy in this moment. With practice I could live in the now all the time. I can't change yesterday, and I can't live tomorrow because it's not here yet. You know, Rocky, you're on to something here.

Thank you, my dear friend. You have taught me so much.

CHAPTER 13

BEING FUNNY LOOKING

"True love is the joy of life." —John Clarke (1596-1658) Comp. Proverbs English and Latin p.26 1639

I f God is love and all he wants you to do is to love yourself and one another, no matter what, then what IS the problem? Somehow, along the way we decided that if someone doesn't look, speak, act, or smell the way we think they should, then for some reason, we treat them differently. I believe God put Funny Looking Animals on earth to teach us that none of us is perfect. **NOT NEAR PERFECT.** When you think of your pet, weren't they perfect? Well, they were perfect because of the LOVE they gave us. Unconditional love. It wasn't how they looked, it was the wonderful feeling you got when you received and gave love back. Hold that thought. Close your eyes and feel the love you gave and received. It is so special, so be sure to embrace that feeling. Now, today, share that feeling with someone who doesn't fit your idea of perfect. You'll be amazed at what you get back.

What do you call a dog with hairless legs that are too long for his body, a back end with no tail, no neck, like Joe Frazier, wonderful pointy ears with lots of beautiful hair coming off every which way, and a smile that brings joy to people's lives. You call him ROCKY, of course. No matter how you looked, which incidentally WAS very funny, you gave love to us that made us feel so special. Normally, you would think that love would only come from humans, but our true teachers are the animals. They have been given a unique quality, and we are the lucky recipients of their love.

Rocky, I have no idea what they are talking about because we thought you were perfect in every way. But it's true. Sometimes, people walking by would stop just to ask what kind of dog you were. Whenever they did, it was always with a smile on their face. You brought joy into people's lives all the time. People would always say how cute you were and really appreciate your special attributes. Do you realize how cute you were?

Some people thought you were an Australian terrier. I'd never seen one so I couldn't say, but in the end we would tell them you were a *"one in a million"* from the Humane Society. They always said the same thing to that answer. They make the best companions! That's what you really were, Rocky. You were the best companion anyone could ever ask for.

CHAPTER 14

APPRECIATION

"Yesterday is but a dream, tomorrow is only a vision. But today, well lived, makes every yesterday a dream of happiness, and every tomorrow a vision of hope. Look well, therefore, to this day, for it is life, the very life of life."
—The Sanskrit

*W*hen you held your pet, when they followed you around the house, when they got underfoot, barely escaping near disaster for you and them, were you thinking how lucky you were to be in that moment? If you could take each little incident, day by day, and create a movie, what would that look like? Can you see yourself appreciating these moments? Take the time right now to reflect back to how much you appreciated everything they contributed to your life. How they gave without any expectation of reward. How can you take this newfound knowledge and share it today?

When I remind myself that I have to appreciate everything I have received in my life, I can remember looking at you, Rocky, and am reminded how uncomplicated you made everything in your life. You never made a big fuss over anything. You took life as it came to you and appreciated what you received.

Every morning when you woke up, life was a clean slate for you. You weren't projecting about the perceived challenges of the day to come. You had perfect trust in whatever was to come. You trusted us to take care of you and we did.

That may seem like an oversimplification, but the fact is you were very cool. With your eyes of wisdom you evaluated every situation and either participated or said, "Not for me," and walked into the other room. You were very good at carving out your own space, and as I look back now, it made you that much more human. Ooops, sorry to call you a human; of course you're a dog. Don't take it personally, but many times your actions certainly had a human quality.

What did you say? Now that is interesting. You understood lots of words like cookie and car, but what you really understood was our body language and tone of voice. Well, that does make a lot of sense. I can clearly remember when dinnertime came around how you would watch all the activity as if we were preparing your dinner. You would follow us around every step, making sure that you would miss nothing. Before we would sit down to eat, we would fix your dinner. I'm sure you were thinking, "Who's that for? I'm going for the good stuff on the plate." Yes, we did share almost every dinner with you, and after we thought you had had enough, you reluctantly retreated to your dinner bowl.

Sorry about that "DOG FOOD," but you **were** incredible healthy your entire life, so we must have done something right. I will say that you did appreciate everything that you did get...thank you.

Hey, Rocky, I saw a TV interview the other day about an animal trainer who claims that she can tell what dogs are thinking...well, not exactly thinking, but she can tell when they are happy or sad. What she said is you can tell when dogs are happy because their mouths are open and their tails are wagging. Thank you, Rocky, you're right, I did know when you were happy, so I appreciate the compliment.

Rocky, you taught me so much about appreciating the moment that I was in. I can close my eyes and remember how wonderful it was to just have you there with me. You would sit with Pam on the sofa and keep her company for as long as she sat there. You were our guardian, our sentinel, our angel.

I also remember how when I got up to go in the other room, you would get up. You were our shadow, and it was comforting to know that you were always keeping an eye out for us. Of course I also know what your other motive was. If there was going to be any dissemination of food, you wanted your share. No matter what, just to have you there was special. Thank you for teaching me so much about appreciation and also for being there in our lives.

At night you would start by sleeping with Pam, curling around her feet to keep you and her warm, but, by the end of the night, you were glued to me. We were locked in our nightly dance of strategic positioning, and each time one of us moved or rolled over, the other would shift to take advantage of new territory. These are memories I will never forget. Oh, by the way, Rocky, I want to apologize to you. Every once in a while when I needed some extra room because you had stolen the covers from me or maneuvered me to the edge of the bed, I would give you a good bump to get you to move. It usually worked to buy me some extra space, but I always felt guilty for waking you up. I don't know why I felt guilty since your primary activity every day was SLEEPING.

Oh well. I hope you will forgive me. But right now as I sit here thinking of you, I wish you were here so we could share one more night together. We miss you. We miss you very, very much.

CHAPTER 15

THE GIFT OF LISTENING

"We have only this moment, sparkling like a star in our hand...and melting like a snowflake. Let us use it before it is too late." —Marie Beynon Ray

I can hear him in the other room. Can you? He's making a noise like he's got his nose in something really interesting. You want to get up and investigate, but no matter what it is, you trust him. WHAT? ARE YOU CRAZY? Get up and go see what he's gotten himself into. You do. It turns out to be some newspaper. Nothing, just some dumb old newspaper. As you pick it up, you notice an article about how a dog saved an entire family when their house caught on fire in the middle of the night, and the dog was able to bark loud enough to get them to wake up. You look at your doggy and start to talk to him about the article. He looks at you with complete comprehension. Have you ever asked yourself why you are talking to your dog? Don't stop. They do understand better than you think.

Rocky, if a dog could become a psychiatrist, you would have made a great one. Of course it would help if you could read, but I truly believe that God gave you all the tools to help people to overcome their challenges.

God gave you the gift of *listening,* and what a gift it was. You were the best listener of all time. Did we ever bore you as we rambled on about the goings on in our lives? You're very kind to say that; you were always fascinated with everything that we said. I know we would look at you and tell you a whole story and at the end of it would say to you, "What do you think, Rocky?" No, I don't think we are unique. I think everyone talks to their pets and uses them as a sounding board. It's kind of like we talk it out with you, and then after verbalizing, it becomes easier for us to make a decision about whatever it was that we were trying to figure out. You were always extremely attentive, and I truly appreciate the fact that you were not so human that you would turn us off and walk away.

I really miss you and the way you would just walk up to me and look up with those big beautiful brown eyes. I have no idea what was on your mind (cookie), but having you there was always a pleasure. You were family, our companion, and we loved you for being a part of our life.

I also know that we used to use you as a buffer between Pam and me. This may sound a little weird, but if we were having trouble communicating with each other or were going through one of those moments, we would talk through you. You know, saying something like, "Did you hear what she said?" I still think lots of people talk through their pets to other people. Are we a little crazy, or is it just sometimes easier to communicate with other people through a pet? I guess it doesn't matter right now, but you are still the best listener there ever was.

No matter what, I really appreciate it that you were always there to listen to us and to help us to communicate better with one another. Thank you, my good friend.

CHAPTER 16

FRIENDSHIP

"There is nothing on earth more to be prized than true friendship."
—Saint Thomas Aquinas

*H*ave *you ever had a friend who you would trust no matter what? Someone you could count on through thick and thin. Someone you could lean on when times were hard.*

Have you ever been that friend?

"A man cannot be said to succeed in this life who does not satisfy one friend."
—Henry David Thoreau

Think about true friendship. It isn't in the receiving that we gain and grow, but rather in the giving do we tap into who we really are. Our pets understand this because they are such great givers. Yes, they are great receivers also, but when the chips are down, you know who you can count on.

Rocky, you have shown me the beauty of friendship. You were always there through thick and thin, and your friendship was never questioned. You know, they say, "Dog is man's best friend." Let's see: unconditional love, never talks back, always has loving eyes, will listen to you for hours on end, will watch TV with you, will eat off the same plate, loves leftovers, and doesn't complain. That's just to name a few of your very special attributes.

Yes, my old friend, I do miss you. You have always been there for me, and for that I will always remember all the fun times that we had. Rolling on the grass, chasing each other in circles, me trying to get you to howl (Owwwwoooo), which you obligingly did, and so many more memorable times that intermittingly come back to me. You will always be with me. Whenever I think of you, it gives you immortality. You are alive in my mind and in my heart, and I feel blessed. Thank you.

CHAPTER 17

GRATEFUL

"I thank you God for this most amazing day; for the leaping greenly spirits of trees and a blue true dream of sky; and for everything which is natural which is infinite which is yes." —e.e. cummings

*H*aving given himself away to the moment, he lay down in the field of wheat moved by a gentle breeze, invisible to all except the passing birds and clouds masquerading as characters from his childhood days. Smelling the sweetness of pines gently wafting their scent, the trees were alive with nature savoring the beauty of the moment, the minute, the hour, the day. Sounds he had never heard before, now, so pronounced and seemingly familiar. He was one with the grass, the trees, the sky, and the life-giving sun as broken rays pierced through branches and leaves, finding their way to warm his soul in the late afternoon of his life. What have I forgotten to remember? he thought to himself. What was it that has escaped me, lingering on the edge of my mind?

Now I remember...thank you for being you. Thank you for being a part of me.

Rocky, in so many ways I have retraced my steps, thinking of all the special moments that you gave me, but there is also the reality that you helped me to see how important it was for me to be grateful every day. In watching you all the years we were together, every day you were so grateful for the life you had with us. As I look back, you were having fun all the time and were comfortable in who you were.

The picture we have of you when you were put up for adoption through the Humane Society, being shown as the "Dog of the Week" tells the whole untold story. You didn't start out your life as a gifted pup. Nobody will ever know how horrific your first year of life was, but the picture tells a story of courage. You were so brave to hang on when hope seemed so distant. You prevailed and as if by a miracle you were saved and found a happy home. I do believe that those early times when your life was so hard helped you find the peace in being grateful every day...and you were. It was through you that we came in touch with the power of counting our blessings every day. You taught us to not only be grateful every morning, but to truly embrace gratitude throughout every day. Thank you, Rocky, for the gifts you unselfishly shared with us throughout your life.

CHAPTER 18

THE RAINBOW

After a while, drifting in and out of thought, living a dream that felt so real, I had an awareness. It was as if I could feel Rocky pressed up against my leg like he always used to do. I reached down with my hand to touch his head, and even though he wasn't there, he was. There was an energy force far greater than anything I had ever felt. It's a fact that everything in the universe is "ENERGY." All people, cars, houses, trees, scrub, roads, light poles, and everything else that has mass on this planet is all "ENERGY." What I mean is everything that exists is made up of molecules and atoms. Before a building was built, it was first an idea in someone's head. They visualized what they wanted to build, and then, using the energy around (building materials), they created the building. If the building materials didn't exist, they created the building materials.

There is energy in the universe, and Rocky's energy was alive and living and sitting at my feet. I knew in my heart that he would not be with me for long as I was sitting there. There is a force greater than all others, and I knew Rocky was being called. His time was precious, and I took this special time to feel his energy for the last time. He came back to me to let me know that everything was OK. He had hung on as long as he could, and just feeling him next to me was reassurance that he was going to be in a new and wonderful place.

As I drifted in my thought, I could hear the ticking of the clock. Tick... tick... tick... but it sounded different to me now. The ticking sounded crisp, almost alive. It was as if, during the time that I had drifted off, time had stopped. I felt refreshed thinking of all the wonderful things Rocky had taught me. I slowly opened my eyes and realized it was still light in the late afternoon. The sun would be setting in another hour, and I felt that I needed to go back up to the beach with Pam to where we had shared our last special moments together with Rocky.

The image was clear in my mind as we stood remembering how he pointed his nose into the breeze and his little legs holding up his beautiful body. He would stop, turn, and look out to the ocean as if he was saying good-bye. We walked down to the water's edge and could feel the energy of the ocean as wave after wave rolled in to greet us and then retreated to deeper water. Rocky stood and stared out to sea and then back at us. He was appreciating the moment just like he always did. I had learned so much from him.

Out in the ocean, probably ten miles or so, was an afternoon shower. We sat next to each other, holding on to one another and remembering how special our little Rocky made us feel. Then as we looked out, we saw something we had not seen in two years. It was a beautiful full color spectrum rainbow, and we could see it touching the ocean at its beginning and end. I felt as though our little Rocky was on the rainbow and headed to heaven. God was calling him, and it was his turn to really go home.

I know that Rocky was on the rainbow and headed to Heaven. God would want Rocky in Heaven because he had such an amazing sense of humor and so much love to share. I'm sure that Rocky will be a beautiful "Doggy Angel." He will be doing all kinds of really important jobs, like comforting people who still miss their families on earth. I can see him curling up on someone's lap, snuggling so close, and helping to relieve their sadness.

We watched the rainbow as it evaporated, leaving us with the beautiful image in our minds. Every time we see a rainbow now, we know that our little Rocky will be running up and down through the colors and greeting new friends.

Rocky, we miss you so very much. Thank you for your lessons.

Printed in the United States
76771LV00003B/208-351